JEST IN TIME: 401 BEST MAN SPEECH JOKES TO KEEP THEM LAUGHING

WIT AND WISDOM FOR THE ULTIMATE WEDDING TOAST

LIGHTHEARTED PUBLISHING

Copyright © 2023 by Lighthearted Publishing

All rights reserved.

No part of this book may be reproduced in any form or by any electronic or mechanical means, including information storage and retrieval systems, without written permission from the author, except for the use of brief quotations in a book review.

INTRODUCTION

∼

Welcome to "Jest in Time: 401 Best Man Speech Jokes to Keep Them Laughing"! Whether you're a seasoned toastmaster or stepping into the spotlight for the first time, this book is your ultimate compendium of humor, wit, and wisdom to make your best man speech truly unforgettable.

Picture this: The big day has arrived, the vows have been exchanged, and now it's your time to shine. The spotlight is on you, and all eyes eagerly await what you have to say. The pressure is on, but fear not, for you hold in your hands the key to delivering a best-man speech that will leave everyone talking, laughing, and praising your comedic prowess.

"Jest in Time" is far more than a collection of jokes—it's a treasure trove of inspiration, guidance, and entertainment. We've meticulously compiled a diverse assortment of jokes, one-liners, and humorous anecdotes that cater to every type of audience and wedding celebration. From the lighthearted and charming to the cheeky and daring, you'll find the perfect blend of humor to keep your listeners engaged and laughing throughout your speech.

But we don't stop there! Along with these side-splitting jests, we provide invaluable tips and tricks to help you weave your newfound arsenal of jokes seamlessly into your speech, strike the right balance between humor and sentiment, and adapt your material to suit the unique personalities of the happy couple and their guests.

So, let "Jest in Time" be your trusty sidekick on this momentous occasion. With our guidance, you'll captivate your audience and create memories that will last a lifetime. Now, are you ready to unleash your inner comedian and deliver a best-man speech for the ages? Let's dive in and get you prepared to steal the show!

401 BEST MAN SPEECH JOKES TO KEEP THEM LAUGHING

∽

1. Marriage is like a game show: sometimes you win big, sometimes you lose, but as long as you're playing together, you'll always have a good time. So, [Bride's Name] and [Groom's Name], get ready to spin the wheel and see what life has in store!
2. They say that marriage is all about teamwork. So, [Groom's Name], when [Bride's Name] asks you to help with the dishes, just remember that you're the point guard, and she's the star shooter. Pass the soap and sink those suds!
3. In marriage, it's important to always have each other's back. So, [Groom's Name], if [Bride's Name] ever needs help reaching something on a high shelf, just remember that you're her personal step ladder.
4. Ladies and gentlemen, let's toast to [Bride's Name] and [Groom's Name]. May their love be like a campfire: warm, cozy, and always ready to roast some marshmallows.

5. Marriage is like a roller coaster: it's thrilling, it's unpredictable, and sometimes you'll feel like you're about to lose your lunch. But as long as you're holding on tight to each other, you'll make it through the ride.
6. They say that in marriage, it's important to laugh together. So, [Groom's Name], when [Bride's Name] tells a joke, just remember to laugh—even if you've heard it a hundred times before!
7. [Groom's Name], a word of advice for a happy marriage: always be prepared to compromise. So when [Bride's Name] asks you to watch a romantic comedy, just remember that there's always a sports game on afterward.
8. In marriage, it's important to always keep the romance alive. So, [Groom's Name], when [Bride's Name] asks for a candlelit dinner, just remember that takeout by candlelight counts, too!
9. Ladies and gentlemen, let's raise a glass to [Bride's Name] and [Groom's Name]. May their love be like a well-choreographed dance: graceful, elegant, and always in perfect sync.
10. Marriage is like a jigsaw puzzle: it takes time, patience, and a keen eye to put all the pieces together. But once it's complete, you'll have a beautiful picture that's worth all the effort.
11. They say that a successful marriage is built on a strong foundation of trust. So, [Groom's Name], when [Bride's Name] asks you to hold her purse, just remember that you've been entrusted with a great responsibility.
12. In marriage, it's important to always be there for each other. So, [Groom's Name], when [Bride's Name] needs a shoulder to cry on, just remember that you're her personal Kleenex.
13. Ladies and gentlemen, let's toast to [Bride's Name] and [Groom's Name]. May their love be like a soaring eagle: majestic, powerful, and always reaching new heights.

14. Marriage is like a treasure hunt: sometimes you'll find gold, sometimes you'll find silver, and sometimes you'll find dirty socks hidden under the bed. But as long as you're searching together, you'll always find something valuable.
15. They say that the key to a happy marriage is to always make time for each other. So, [Groom's Name], when [Bride's Name] asks for a date night, just remember that you can always reschedule that video game tournament.
16. In marriage, it's important to always be honest with each other. So, [Groom's Name], when [Bride's Name] asks for your opinion on her new haircut, just remember to choose your words carefully!
17. Ladies and gentlemen, let's raise a glass to [Bride's Name] and [Groom's Name]. May their love be like a well-written novel: full of adventure, romance, and always leaving you wanting more.
18. Marriage is like a sports team: it takes practice, dedication, and sometimes a little bit of coaching to be successful. So, [Bride's Name] and [Groom's Name], always be ready to huddle up and work on your game plan together.
19. They say that in marriage, it's important to keep the spark alive. So, [Groom's Name], when [Bride's Name] asks for a romantic getaway, just remember that a camping trip with a cozy fire can be just as romantic as a five-star hotel.
20. In marriage, it's important to always support each other's dreams. So, [Groom's Name], when [Bride's Name] decides to take up skydiving, just remember to be her personal cheerleader and pack her parachute with care!
21. Ladies and gentlemen, let's toast to [Bride's Name] and [Groom's Name]. May their love be like a well-tended vineyard: always producing the finest of wines and aging to perfection.
22. Marriage is like a marathon: it takes endurance, perseverance, and sometimes a little bit of chafing. But as

long as you're running together, you'll always cross the finish line hand in hand.

23. They say that the secret to a long and happy marriage is to always keep learning and growing together. So, [Groom's Name], when [Bride's Name] signs you both up for salsa dancing lessons, just remember to put on your dancing shoes and be ready to cha-cha-cha your way to marital bliss.
24. In marriage, it's important to always be each other's biggest fan. So, [Groom's Name], when [Bride's Name] decides to take up knitting, just remember to wear that homemade scarf with pride!
25. Ladies and gentlemen, let's raise a glass to [Bride's Name] and [Groom's Name]. May their love be like a symphony: full of passion, harmony, and always striking the right chord.
26. I always thought the groom was the luckiest man in the room, until I saw the line for the open bar.
27. As the best man, it's my job to make sure the groom doesn't do anything he'll regret... like getting married.
28. I want to start by thanking the groom for finally settling down and giving the rest of us a chance.
29. If the bride and groom are the happiest couple in the world, then I must be the happiest person in this room... I'm not the one getting married!
30. I asked the groom how he knew the bride was the one, and he said, "She's the only one who could put up with my jokes."
31. It's been said that marriage is like a deck of cards: you start with two hearts and a diamond, but by the end, you're looking for a club and a spade.
32. When the bride and groom asked me to be the best man, I said, "Of course! I have nothing better to do on a Saturday night."

33. I'm not saying the groom is a cheap date, but he only proposed to the bride because she said yes to splitting the bill.
34. I know the bride and groom are meant to be together because they both have the same password on their phones: "I love you."
35. If you're ever feeling down, just remember: at least you're not the one giving the best man speech.
36. Marriage is a lot like a game of chess: it takes strategy, patience, and the ability to say "checkmate" without gloating.
37. The groom's bachelor party was so wild he woke up with a tattoo of the bride's name... luckily, it was spelled right.
38. If the bride and groom were a movie, they'd be a romantic comedy... because they're both so damn funny.
39. I'm honored to be the best man, but I'm a little disappointed I didn't get to be the ring bearer. Those pillow fights look like a lot of fun.
40. I asked the bride and groom if they had any advice for me on my own love life, and they said, "Don't take advice from us."
41. Marriage is a lot like a rollercoaster: there are ups and downs, twists and turns, and sometimes you just want to scream your head off.
42. The bride and groom are the perfect match: she's the peanut butter to his jelly, the salt to his pepper, and the hangover cure to his late-night drinking.
43. As the best man, it's my job to make sure the groom is always on his toes... which is why I replaced his dress shoes with roller skates.
44. The bride and groom have been together for so long, they're practically a vintage item... like a classic car or a retro toaster.

45. I asked the groom if he had any pre-wedding jitters, and he said, "Only about giving the best man speech." Well, buddy, you're on your own for that one.
46. The groom is a lucky guy - he gets to wake up every day next to the most beautiful person in the world... himself.
47. I've known the groom for so long that I've watched him go through more girlfriends than Taylor Swift.
48. Marriage is a lot like a game of football: you need to have a good game plan, you'll face some tough opponents, and there will be a lot of cheering and high-fives when you finally score.
49. The bride and groom are like two peas in a pod... except the pod is a little bigger now.
50. I'm here to make a toast to the happy couple, but let's be honest - they don't need any more alcohol to be happy.
51. The bride and groom are like a pair of shoes - they may not look like a perfect match at first, but they fit together perfectly.
52. The groom may be losing his bachelor status, but he's gaining a partner for life, a companion, and a new roommate... who will always leave the toilet seat down.
53. The best man's speech is a lot like a mini-skirt: it should be long enough to cover the important parts but short enough to keep it interesting.
54. The groom may have found the love of his life, but he still hasn't found a solution to his snoring.
55. The bride and groom are like two puzzle pieces that fit perfectly together, except they never seem to know where the other one is.
56. They say marriage is a journey, and the bride and groom are off to a great start with a honeymoon in Hawaii... or at least that's what the groom thinks.
57. The bride and groom have been through so much together - they've weathered storms, climbed mountains, and even survived a few rounds of Monopoly.

58. The groom is like a fish that's been caught - he's hooked for life, but at least he's with the one he loves.
59. The bride and groom are like two peas in a pod, but hopefully, they won't end up like those two peas that always get stuck in your teeth.
60. As the best man, I have to admit I'm a little jealous of the groom - he's marrying the most amazing person in the world, and I'm stuck giving a speech.
61. The bride and groom are like two sides of a coin - they may be different, but together they make a great team.
62. Marriage is a lot like a garden: you need to plant the seeds, water them regularly, and if you're lucky, you'll have a beautiful and fruitful garden for years to come.
63. I've never seen the groom so nervous as when he was picking out his wedding outfit... but to be fair, he's been wearing the same hoodie for the past 5 years.
64. The bride and groom may have different hobbies and interests, but they both love each other more than anything... except maybe pizza.
65. I asked the groom what he was most excited about on his wedding day, and he said, "Finally getting to take off this damn tuxedo."
66. Ladies and gentlemen, before I begin, the bride and groom have asked me to request that you please place any gifts you've brought on the table by the exit. And if you haven't brought a gift, there's still time to run to the ATM.
67. For those of you who don't know me, I'm [Your Name], the best man, and I'm here to tell you about the groom. But don't worry, I've been strictly instructed to keep this speech rated PG-13, so all the really good stories will have to wait for the afterparty.
68. I've known [Groom's Name] for a long time, and I've been asked on several occasions how we became friends. It's simple, really—we bonded over our shared inability to

dance. Luckily for the bride, he's been taking secret lessons in preparation for tonight.

69. A wise man once said that a successful marriage is about falling in love many times, always with the same person. In [Groom's Name] and [Bride's Name]'s case, I think they've already hit that number just during the wedding planning process.

70. It's said that the secret to a happy marriage is communication. So, [Groom's Name], when [Bride's Name] says, "we need to talk," remember that's code for "I need to talk, you need to listen."

71. I must say, [Bride's Name], you look absolutely stunning today. And [Groom's Name], well, you look... stunned.

72. People say that marriage is like a roller coaster. There are ups and downs, thrills and chills. But as long as you're holding on tight to each other, you'll enjoy the ride together. Just remember, [Groom's Name], screaming is allowed on roller coasters, not during wedding speeches.

73. They say you don't marry someone you can live with; you marry someone you can't live without. And judging by how often [Groom's Name] talks about [Bride's Name], I can safely say he's found that person.

74. I've been told that in marriage, it's important to have a sense of humor. And since [Groom's Name] has been laughing at his own jokes for years, I think he's well-prepared.

75. In closing, I'd like to share some advice that's been passed down through generations: A happy wife makes a happy life. So, [Groom's Name], if you can remember those words and act accordingly, you'll have a lifetime of happiness ahead of you.

76. Ladies and gentlemen, today we're not only celebrating the union of [Bride's Name] and [Groom's Name] but also their very first day of forming a new company: [Bride's

Name] & [Groom's Name] Incorporated. Their slogan? "Together, we're one heck of a merger."

77. [Groom's Name], they say a good marriage is like a good wine—it only gets better with age. So, remember, when you're both old and wrinkly, you'll be vintage!

78. I've always heard that love is a lot like a game of cards: You start out with two hearts and a diamond, and by the end, you're just looking for a club and a spade.

79. I asked [Groom's Name] what he was most looking forward to about married life, and he said, "Finally having someone to share the remote control with." I'm just not sure if he realizes that sharing means [Bride's Name] gets to use it too.

80. I've been told that a great marriage is like a duck: It looks calm and smooth on the surface, but underneath, there's a whole lot of frantic paddling. So, here's to [Bride's Name] and [Groom's Name]—may you paddle together in perfect harmony!

81. Ladies and gentlemen, the bride and groom have requested that I not share any embarrassing stories about [Groom's Name] today. Fortunately for you, they didn't say anything about embarrassing photos. So, feel free to swing by my table during the reception for a private viewing.

82. During my research for this speech, I came across an old proverb that says, "A man in love is incomplete until he's married. Then he's finished." But knowing [Groom's Name], I think he's just getting started on this incredible journey with [Bride's Name].

83. They say that love is blind, but marriage is an eye-opener. So, [Groom's Name], I hope you're ready to see [Bride's Name]'s extensive collection of shoes and handbags.

84. I recently learned that in ancient times, people believed that once you got married, your two souls became one. If that's true, then [Groom's Name], congratulations—you've just doubled your wardrobe!

85. Marriage is a lot like a roller coaster: It has its ups and downs, but as long as you're sitting next to the right person, you can enjoy the ride. And if you're wondering how to spot the right person, just remember: They're the one screaming with you, not at you.
86. Marriage is like a team sport: it takes cooperation, dedication, and sometimes a little bit of coaching. But as long as you're playing together, you'll always be on the winning team.
87. They say that behind every great man, there's a great woman rolling her eyes. So, [Groom's Name], get ready for a lifetime of expert eye-rolls from [Bride's Name].
88. To help [Groom's Name] prepare for married life, I gave him a book titled "The Man's Guide to a Happy Marriage." It's just one page long and says, "Yes, dear."
89. Now that [Bride's Name] and [Groom's Name] are married, they'll be taking on new roles. [Bride's Name] will be the chef, the cleaner, and the organizer, while [Groom's Name] will be... well, grateful.
90. I asked [Groom's Name] if he knew the secret to a long, happy marriage. He said, "Two words: separate bathrooms."
91. Ladies and gentlemen, if you want to know the real secret to a happy marriage, it's this: Always remember the three little words that can diffuse any argument – "You're right, dear."
92. [Groom's Name] told me he's excited about married life because it means he'll always have someone to lean on. Little does he know, [Bride's Name] is already planning on leaning on him too—especially when it's time to take out the trash.
93. I was told that when you marry someone, you marry their whole family. So, [Groom's Name], congratulations on your beautiful new bride and her 27 cousins, who all need a place to stay this weekend!

94. They say the key to a happy marriage is compromise. In other words, [Groom's Name], get ready to watch a lot of romantic comedies.
95. [Bride's Name] and [Groom's Name], I wish you a lifetime of love, laughter, and endless happiness. And if you ever need help with your taxes, I'll be there for you—just like I was there for [Groom's Name] when he tried to claim his dog as a dependent.
96. [Groom's Name], I have some advice for you: If, at first, you don't succeed, try doing it the way your wife told you to.
97. You know what they say about weddings—something old, something new, something borrowed, and something blue. Well, [Bride's Name], today you've got something old (your loving parents), something new (your stunning dress), something borrowed (that fabulous necklace), and something blue... (the look on [Groom's Name]'s face when he sees the wedding bill).
98. A wise man once told me that marriage is like a workshop. The husband works, and the wife shops!
99. They say the secret to a successful marriage is to treat it like a job. So, [Groom's Name], congratulations on your promotion to "Husband"—it comes with a lifetime contract!
100. Ladies and gentlemen, if you're wondering why [Bride's Name] and [Groom's Name] look so perfect together, it's because opposites attract. She's organized, he's messy; she's punctual, he's always late; she's got great taste, and well, she married him.
101. In preparing for this speech, I did some research and found that a happy marriage requires patience, understanding, and a well-stocked liquor cabinet.
102. [Groom's Name] told me he was nervous about this whole marriage thing, so I shared some reassuring words: "Don't worry, buddy, getting married is a piece of cake. Just

remember, it's the first bite of many servings of humble pie."

103. People always say that a perfect marriage is one where the husband is the head and the wife is the neck. So, [Groom's Name], remember that the neck can always turn the head in whichever direction it pleases.

104. I've been told that a happy marriage is like a good game of chess: The queen always protects her king. So, [Groom's Name], you're in good hands with [Bride's Name]—just don't make any illegal moves!

105. Marriage is a lot like a fine wine: It's fruity, complex, and sometimes gives you a headache. But in the end, it's always worth it.

106. Ladies and gentlemen, today we celebrate a beautiful union. It's the perfect combination, much like peanut butter and jelly, cookies, and milk, or [Groom's Name] and his video game console.

107. Here's some advice for the newlyweds: A successful marriage is built on trust, love, and a reliable Wi-Fi connection.

108. They say the key to a long, happy marriage is a good sense of humor. So, [Groom's Name], if you're ever in trouble, just remember to laugh at [Bride's Name]'s jokes—even the ones that aren't funny.

109. Marriage is like a roller coaster. Sometimes you're on top of the world, and other times you're stuck in the dark, wondering why you ever got on this crazy ride. But one thing's for sure: It's never boring!

110. They say you can tell a lot about a person by the company they keep. In that case, [Bride's Name], I have to say—you could have done a lot better than [Groom's Name].

111. I've heard that the secret to a happy marriage is a short memory. So, [Groom's Name], if you ever forget [Bride's Name]'s birthday or anniversary, just remember this

helpful tip: You probably won't be married for much longer!

112. [Groom's Name], I hope you're ready for a lifetime of romantic gestures because, in marriage, actions speak louder than words. And when I say actions, I mean doing the dishes, taking out the trash, and putting the toilet seat down.

113. A great marriage is like a good cup of coffee: strong, hot, and full of energy. But if it goes cold, there's always the microwave to heat things back up!

114. Ladies and gentlemen, we've all heard that love is a journey, not a destination. Well, I hope [Bride's Name] and [Groom's Name] have packed their bags because they're about to embark on the wildest adventure of their lives!

115. They say that in marriage, you should never go to bed angry. So, [Groom's Name], I hope you're ready for some very late nights and very long conversations.

116. The groom may have given up his freedom, but he's gaining something much more valuable - a lifetime supply of love and companionship.

117. The bride and groom are like a pair of shoes - they may have different styles, but together they make a complete outfit.

118. They say marriage is all about compromise, but I think the groom compromised a little more than the bride did.

119. The bride and groom have been together for so long that they know each other better than they know themselves... which is probably why they're getting married.

120. I'm not saying the groom is whipped, but he did propose on one knee and with a bouquet of flowers.

121. Marriage is like a marathon, and the bride and groom have just crossed the starting line... with a wedding cake in hand.

122. The bride and groom are like two pieces of a puzzle - they may not fit perfectly at first, but with a little effort, they come together beautifully.
123. As the best man, it's my job to make sure the groom doesn't embarrass himself on his wedding day... but I'm not sure I can do anything about those dance moves.
124. The bride and groom are like two sides of a coin - they may have different personalities, but together they make a great team.
125. They say marriage is all about finding the right person - but in this case, the bride and groom found each other by accident.
126. The groom may be getting married, but his bachelor party will live on forever in our memories... and the photos on social media.
127. The bride and groom are like two peas in a pod - they go together so well that it's almost annoying.
128. As the best man, I'm supposed to make the groom look good... but I'm not sure there's much I can do about that haircut.
129. Marriage is like a road trip - there will be bumps in the road, but as long as you have the right company, it'll be a great adventure.
130. The bride and groom are like a pair of headphones - they may have different sounds, but together they make beautiful music.
131. As the best man, I have a few embarrassing stories about the groom... but I promised his mom I wouldn't share them.
132. Marriage is like a rollercoaster - there will be highs and lows, but as long as you hold on tight, it'll be a wild ride.
133. The bride and groom are like two pieces of a puzzle - they may have different strengths and weaknesses, but together they create a perfect picture.

134. They say love is blind, but the bride and groom clearly have 20/20 vision... because they found each other.
135. As the best man, I have to admit that the groom has always been the better dancer... but I'm still going to embarrass him on the dance floor.
136. Marriage is like a game of cards - you have to know when to hold 'em, know when to fold 'em and know when to ask your spouse for advice.
137. The bride and groom may have different tastes in music, but they both love each other's playlists... or at least they pretend to.
138. The groom may be nervous about his wedding day, but I'm more worried about his choice of best man.
139. The bride and groom are like two ingredients in a recipe - they may not seem like a perfect match, but together they make something amazing.
140. Marriage is like a garden - you have to tend to it every day, and if you're lucky, it'll bloom into something beautiful.
141. The bride and groom are like two peas in a pod - they may be annoyingly perfect together, but at least they're not.
142. The groom may be losing his freedom, but he's gaining someone to blame when he forgets important dates and events.
143. The bride and groom are like a pair of shoes - they may have different sizes, but together they make a perfect fit.
144. Marriage is like a dance - sometimes it's slow and romantic, and sometimes it's a crazy and wild party.
145. The bride and groom are like two different flavors of ice cream - they may be different, but together they create the perfect sundae.
146. As the best man, it's my job to make sure the groom looks good on his wedding day... which is why I'm not letting him near the cake.

147. Marriage is like a puzzle - it may take some time and effort, but once you put all the pieces together, you get a beautiful picture.
148. The bride and groom are like two different sides of a coin - they may have different personalities, but they share the same love.
149. As the best man, I have to say the groom is a lucky guy - he's getting a lifetime supply of love, affection, and home-cooked meals.
150. Marriage is like a journey - sometimes it's smooth sailing, and sometimes it's a bumpy ride, but it's always an adventure.
151. The bride and groom are like two different ingredients in a recipe - they may seem odd together, but they create something delicious.
152. As the best man, it's my job to make sure the groom doesn't make any mistakes on his wedding day... but I can't do anything about those hair plugs.
153. Marriage is like a game of chess - you have to think ahead, plan your moves carefully, and sometimes sacrifice a pawn for the greater good.
154. The bride and groom are like two different pieces of a puzzle - they may not fit perfectly, but together they make a beautiful picture.
155. As the best man, I have to admit the groom has always been the better-looking one... but I still have a better sense of humor.
156. Marriage is like a book - you never know how it will end, but you're excited to see what happens in the next chapter.
157. The bride and groom are like two different colors - they may not match perfectly, but together they create a beautiful palette.
158. As the best man, it's my job to make sure the groom doesn't do anything stupid on his wedding day... but I can't do anything about that embarrassing tattoo.

159. Marriage is like a garden - you have to water it, prune it, and give it lots of love, but it'll bloom into something beautiful.
160. The bride and groom are like two different instruments - they may sound different, but together they make beautiful music.
161. As the best man, I have to admit the groom has always been the cooler one... but I still have more hair.
162. Marriage is like a game of tennis - you have to work together, communicate, and have each other's back, but the goal is always to win.
163. The bride and groom are like two different pieces of a puzzle - they may seem incompatible, but together they create a beautiful work of art.
164. As the best man, it's my job to make sure the groom has the best wedding day possible... but I can't do anything about the weather.
165. Marriage is like a recipe - you have to mix together different ingredients, add some spice, and sometimes improvise, but the result is always delicious.
166. The bride and groom are like two different flowers - they may be unique, but together they make a beautiful bouquet.
167. As the best man, I have to say the groom is a lucky guy - he's marrying the woman of his dreams, and he didn't even have to swipe right.
168. Marriage is like a road trip - you never know what you're going to encounter, but as long as you're together, you'll have a great time.
169. The bride and groom are like two different spices - they may be different, but together they make a delicious dish.
170. As the best man, I have to admit that the groom has always been the better athlete... but I still have more trophies.
171. They say that marriage is like a rollercoaster – you'll have your ups and downs, twists and turns. But [Groom's

Name], with [Bride's Name] by your side, at least you'll never have to wait in line for the next ride!

172. The bride and groom are like two different beverages - they may be different, but together they make a refreshing cocktail.
173. As the best man, it's my job to make sure the groom looks his best on his wedding day... which is why I'm not letting him near the scissors.
174. Marriage is like a painting - you have to add different colors, layers, and textures, but the final result is always beautiful.
175. The bride and groom are like two different spices - they may not seem like a good match, but together they make a perfect blend.
176. As the best man, I have to say the groom is a lucky guy - he's marrying the woman of his dreams, and he didn't even have to go on a dating app.
177. Marriage is like a game of basketball - you have to work together, pass the ball, and score as a team.
178. The bride and groom are like two different puzzle pieces - they may not fit together at first, but with time and effort, they create a beautiful picture.
179. As the best man, it's my job to make sure the groom doesn't do anything stupid on his wedding day... which is why I'm keeping him away from the karaoke machine.
180. Marriage is like a garden - you have to sow the seeds, water them, and give them lots of sunshine, but the result is always a beautiful and bountiful harvest.
181. The bride and groom are like two different musical instruments - they may sound different, but together they make beautiful music.
182. As the best man, I have to say the groom is a lucky guy - he's marrying someone who loves him despite his dad jokes.

183. Marriage is like a game of soccer - you have to work together, pass the ball, and score goals as a team.
184. The bride and groom are like two different fabrics - they may be different, but together they make a beautiful and unique outfit.
185. As the best man, it's my job to make sure the groom doesn't have any pre-wedding jitters... which is why I'm bringing him a shot of tequila.
186. Marriage is like a work of art - you have to add different colors, shapes, and textures, but the final result is always beautiful.
187. The bride and groom are like two different spices - they may be different, but together they create a unique and delicious flavor.
188. As the best man, I have to say the groom is a lucky guy - he's marrying someone who loves him despite his terrible taste in music.
189. Marriage is like a game of tennis - you have to work together, communicate, and have each other's back, but the goal is always to win.
190. The bride and groom are like two different plants - they may be different, but together they create a beautiful and thriving garden.
191. As the best man, it's my job to make sure the groom doesn't embarrass himself during his speech... but I can't do anything about his dad dancing.
192. Marriage is like a symphony - you have to add different instruments, melodies, and rhythms, but together they create beautiful music.
193. The bride and groom are like two different pieces of artwork - they may be different, but together they create a beautiful and unique collection.
194. As the best man, I have to say the groom is a lucky guy - he's marrying someone who loves him despite his strange obsession with collecting comic books.

195. Marriage is like a game of chess - you have to strategize, make sacrifices, and protect your queen, but in the end, it's all worth it.
196. The bride and groom are like two different elements - they may be different, but together they create a powerful and beautiful bond.
197. As the best man, it's my job to make sure the groom doesn't forget his wedding vows... but I can't do anything about his terrible memory.
198. Marriage is like a puzzle - you have to find the right pieces, fit them together, and create a beautiful picture.
199. The bride and groom are like two different flavors of ice cream - they may be different, but together they create the perfect scoop.
200. As the best man, I have to admit the groom has always been the smarter one... but I still have a better sense of direction.
201. Marriage is like a journey - you never know where it will take you, but as long as you're together, it's always an adventure.
202. The bride and groom are like two different parts of a whole - they may be different, but together they create a perfect balance.
203. As the best man, it's my job to make sure the groom doesn't get too emotional during the ceremony... but I can't do anything about his sentimental side.
204. Marriage is like a puzzle - you have to find the right pieces, fit them together, and create a beautiful picture.
205. The bride and groom are like two different spices - they may be different, but together they create a perfect blend of flavors.
206. As the best man, I have to say the groom is a lucky guy - he's marrying someone who loves him despite his terrible taste in movies.

207. Marriage is like a game of football - you have to work together, tackle obstacles, and score touchdowns as a team.
208. The bride and groom are like two different notes - they may be different, but together they create a beautiful melody.
209. As the best man, it's my job to make sure the groom doesn't drink too much on his wedding day... but I can't do anything about his love for beer.
210. Marriage is like a work of art - you have to add different colors, shapes, and textures, but the final result is always beautiful.
211. The bride and groom are like two different pieces of furniture - they may be different, but together they create a perfect home.
212. As the best man, I have to admit the groom has always been the more stylish one... but I still have better taste in music.
213. Marriage is like a journey - you never know what's ahead, but as long as you're together, you can conquer anything.
214. The bride and groom are like two different ingredients - they may be different, but together they create a delicious and unique recipe.
215. As the best man, I have to say the groom is a lucky guy - he's marrying someone who loves him despite his embarrassing dance moves.
216. Marriage is like a fine dining experience: you start with the appetizers, move on to the main course, and finish with dessert. Just remember, [Groom's Name], there's no such thing as "all-you-can-eat" in marriage, so savor every moment!
217. You know what they say: The couple that laughs together stays together. So, [Bride's Name] and [Groom's Name], here's to a lifetime of laughter, love, and never having to laugh at your own jokes again.

218. A wise man once said, "Marriage is a relationship in which one person is always right, and the other is the husband."
219. [Groom's Name], I have some advice for you: A happy wife is a happy life. A mad wife is... well, let's just say you'd better start sleeping with one eye open.
220. In marriage, it's important to pick your battles wisely. For example, [Groom's Name], you may want to let [Bride's Name] win the argument about the color of the living room walls, but be prepared to fight to the death over control of the TV remote.
221. They say that marriage is like an amusement park ride: sometimes it's thrilling, sometimes it's terrifying, but at the end of the day, you're just happy you didn't throw up.
222. [Bride's Name] and [Groom's Name], I wish you a lifetime of love, laughter, and endless happiness. And if you ever need help assembling IKEA furniture, just remember that I'm only a phone call away!
223. Here's a tip for the newlyweds: In marriage, it's important to have a good sense of humor. But remember, [Groom's Name], there's a time and a place for everything—especially your dad jokes.
224. Marriage is a lot like a jigsaw puzzle: It takes patience, dedication, and sometimes you have to force the pieces to fit together.
225. [Groom's Name], always remember that in marriage, it's important to be flexible. That way, when [Bride's Name] asks you to do yoga with her, you'll be prepared.
226. They say that the secret to a successful marriage is learning to compromise. So, [Groom's Name], you might want to start practicing by letting [Bride's Name] choose the restaurant for date night.
227. Marriage is like a roller coaster: It has its ups and downs, but if you can hang on tight and scream together, you'll make it through the ride.

228. Ladies and gentlemen, did you know that love is like a game of poker? You start with a pair, and if you're lucky, you'll end up with a full house!
229. A great marriage is like a campfire: It takes a little work to get it started, but once it's burning brightly, it'll keep you warm and cozy all night long.
230. Ladies and gentlemen, let's raise a glass to [Bride's Name] and [Groom's Name]. May their love be like a gentle breeze: refreshing, comforting, and always there when you need it.
231. Marriage is like a box of chocolates: you never know what you're going to get. But with [Bride's Name] and [Groom's Name], I think it's safe to say we're in for a treat!
232. You know what they say: A good marriage is like a casserole—only those responsible for it really know what goes into it.
233. In marriage, it's important to find someone who can make you laugh, who can make you think, and who can make you a sandwich when you're too tired to do it yourself. Congratulations, [Groom's Name], you've found your perfect match in [Bride's Name]!
234. Ladies and gentlemen, let's raise a toast to [Bride's Name] and [Groom's Name]. May their love be like a fine wine—getting better with age and never going sour!
235. A successful marriage is all about communication. So, [Groom's Name], when [Bride's Name] says she's "fine," just remember that it's code for "you'd better figure out what's wrong, and fast!"
236. They say the key to a successful marriage is to always remember the three C's: Communication, Compromise, and... Chocolate. Lots of chocolate.
237. Ladies and gentlemen, [Groom's Name] and [Bride's Name] are a perfect match. Just like salt and pepper, ketchup and mustard, or Netflix and chill.

238. [Groom's Name], remember that a happy marriage is all about teamwork. You cook, she eats; you wash, she dries; you watch the game, she... well, maybe not everything is a team effort!
239. Marriage is a lot like a bank account: you put in, you take out, and sometimes you lose interest. But with [Bride's Name] and [Groom's Name], I have a feeling their love account will always be overflowing.
240. [Groom's Name], when you said "I do," you didn't just gain a wife—you gained a personal stylist, a life coach, and a new boss. Congrats on the upgrade!
241. They say that in marriage, you should always put your spouse first. So, [Groom's Name], from now on, you'll need to make sure [Bride's Name]'s coffee is ready before you even think about making your own.
242. [Groom's Name], a word of advice: In marriage, it's important to admit when you're wrong. But when you're right... just stay quiet and enjoy the moment.
243. Ladies and gentlemen here's to [Bride's Name] and [Groom's Name]—a couple who've found the secret to eternal happiness: low expectations and a great sense of humor!
244. In marriage, it's important to be a good listener. So, [Groom's Name], when [Bride's Name] starts talking about her day, be sure to nod, smile, and occasionally say, "Wow, that's crazy!" Trust me, it works.
245. Did you know that marriage is like a seesaw? It takes two people working together to find the perfect balance. Just don't push too hard, or someone might end up on the ground!
246. Marriage is like a marathon: it's long, challenging, and sometimes painful, but crossing the finish line together makes it all worth it.
247. They say that the secret to a long and happy marriage is to never stop dating... each other, of course!

248. [Groom's Name], I hope you're ready for a lifetime of surprises because marriage is like a box of chocolates: sometimes you get the sweet ones, and sometimes you get the ones filled with toothpaste.
249. Ladies and gentlemen, let's raise a toast to [Bride's Name] and [Groom's Name]. May their marriage be like a well-oiled machine, running smoothly and efficiently, with only the occasional need for maintenance.
250. Marriage is like a garden: it takes a lot of work, patience, and fertilizer to make it grow. So, [Groom's Name], be prepared to get your hands dirty!
251. They say that a successful marriage is built on trust, love, and a mutual appreciation for each other's quirks. So, [Groom's Name], get ready to start loving [Bride's Name]'s obsession with cat videos!
252. Marriage is like a roller coaster: you'll experience twists and turns, ups and downs, and moments when you want to scream. But at the end of the ride, you'll always be glad you took the plunge together.
253. In marriage, it's important to remember the three A's: Affection, Appreciation, and... Alibi. Because sometimes you need a partner in crime who can vouch for your whereabouts!
254. Ladies and gentlemen, let's raise a glass to [Bride's Name] and [Groom's Name]. May their love be like a well-tuned orchestra, always in harmony and making beautiful music together.
255. They say that marriage is like a roller coaster, and the secret to enjoying the ride is to hold on tight and scream together. So, [Bride's Name] and [Groom's Name], get ready for the ride of your lives!
256. Marriage is like a book: there are good chapters, bad chapters, and sometimes you'll find a plot twist you never saw coming. But when you reach the end, you'll be glad you read the whole story.

257. In marriage, it's important to have a backup plan. So, [Groom's Name], if you ever forget [Bride's Name]'s birthday, just remember that flowers, chocolates, and an apology go a long way!

258. They say that marriage is like a fine wine: it gets better with age. But don't worry, [Groom's Name]—even if you're more of a beer guy, I'm sure [Bride's Name] will age gracefully for both of you.

259. Ladies and gentlemen, let's toast to [Bride's Name] and [Groom's Name]. May their love be like a well-tailored suit: stylish, comfortable, and always the perfect fit.

260. Marriage is like a game of poker: sometimes you need to bluff, sometimes you need to fold, and sometimes you just have to go all in. But remember, [Groom's Name], always play your cards right with [Bride's Name].

261. They say that in marriage, it's important to learn to dance in the rain. So, [Bride's Name] and [Groom's Name], grab your umbrellas and start practicing your moves!

262. [Groom's Name], a word of advice: In marriage, it's important to be flexible. So when [Bride's Name] asks you to join her for a yoga class, remember to say yes and start practicing your downward dog.

263. Marriage is like a roller coaster: sometimes it's exhilarating, sometimes it's terrifying, but as long as you're holding hands, you'll make it through together.

264. A successful marriage is all about balance. So, [Groom's Name], if you're going to spend all day watching sports, be prepared to spend your evenings binge-watching [Bride's Name]'s favorite TV shows.

265. Ladies and gentlemen, let's raise a glass to [Bride's Name] and [Groom's Name]. May their love be like a fine piece of art: captivating, inspiring, and always worth admiring.

266. In marriage, it's important to share the responsibilities. So, [Groom's Name], when it's time to do the laundry, just

remember: you wash, [Bride's Name] dries, and you both fold!

267. They say that in marriage, you should always put your best foot forward. So, [Groom's Name], I hope you've invested in some good-quality socks.

268. [Groom's Name], a word of advice for a happy marriage: never underestimate the power of a well-timed compliment. So, when [Bride's Name] asks how she looks, always remember to say, "Absolutely stunning!"

269. Marriage is like a road trip: sometimes there are detours, sometimes there are flat tires, but as long as you're traveling together, you'll always reach your destination.

270. They say that a successful marriage is built on a foundation of love, trust, and a shared Netflix password. So, [Bride's Name] and [Groom's Name], here's to endless movie nights and binge-watching your favorite shows together!

271. In marriage, it's important to always be honest. But, [Groom's Name], when [Bride's Name] asks if her cooking is better than your mom's, remember that sometimes a little white lie can go a long way.

272. Marriage is like a team sport: it takes dedication, hard work, and a little bit of luck to score the winning goal. So, [Bride's Name] and [Groom's Name], lace up your cleats and get ready to play the game of your lives!

273. Ladies and gentlemen, let's toast to [Bride's Name] and [Groom's Name]. May their love be like a lighthouse: strong, bright, and guiding them through even the stormiest of seas.

274. They say that marriage is like a puzzle: it takes time, patience, and a little bit of trial and error to put all the pieces together. But once it's complete, you'll have a beautiful picture that's worth all the effort.

275. Marriage is like a game of chess: you have to think several moves ahead, protect your queen, and sometimes sacrifice

a few pawns to win the game. Just remember, [Groom's Name], always play smart and keep [Bride's Name] out of check!

276. In marriage, it's important to be prepared for the unexpected. So, [Groom's Name], when [Bride's Name] comes home with a new pet, just remember to smile, nod, and start brainstorming names.

277. They say that a successful marriage is all about give and take. So, [Bride's Name], be prepared to give [Groom's Name] the remote, and [Groom's Name], be prepared to take out the trash!

278. Marriage is like a roller coaster: it's full of twists, turns, and sometimes you'll feel like you're upside down. But as long as you're holding on tight to each other, you'll enjoy the ride.

279. Ladies and gentlemen, let's raise a glass to [Bride's Name] and [Groom's Name]. May their love be like a well-tended garden: always growing, blooming, and filled with beauty.

280. They say that the secret to a long and happy marriage is to always say "I love you" before going to bed. And if you're really smart, [Groom's Name], you'll say it first thing in the morning, too!

281. Marriage is like a game of golf - you have to be patient, take your time, and always aim for the hole.

282. The bride and groom are like two different books - they may be different, but together they create a beautiful and inspiring story.

283. As the best man, it's my job to make sure the groom doesn't get too emotional during his vows... but I can't do anything about those tears.

284. Marriage is like a puzzle - sometimes, the pieces fit perfectly, and sometimes you have to force them together to make them work.

285. The bride and groom are like two different types of tea - they may be different, but together they create a perfect blend of flavors.
286. As the best man, I have to admit the groom has always been the more successful one... but I still have a better sense of humor.
287. Marriage is like a game of cards - you have to play your hand carefully, know when to fold, and always have a few tricks up your sleeve.
288. The bride and groom are like two different colors - they may be different, but together they create a beautiful and vibrant painting.
289. As the best man, it's my job to make sure the groom doesn't forget his wedding ring... but I can't do anything about his forgetfulness.
290. Marriage is like a dance - sometimes it's slow and romantic, and sometimes it's a wild and crazy party.
291. The bride and groom are like two different flowers - they may be different, but together they create a beautiful and fragrant bouquet.
292. As the best man, I have to admit the groom has always been the more athletic one... but I still have better hair.
293. Marriage is like a game of chess - you have to plan your moves carefully, think ahead, and always protect your queen.
294. The bride and groom are like two different ingredients - they may be different, but together they create a delicious and unique recipe.
295. As the best man, it's my job to make sure the groom doesn't have any wardrobe malfunctions... but I can't do anything about those shoes.
296. Marriage is like a road trip - you have to be prepared for anything, expect the unexpected, and always have a good playlist.

297. The bride and groom are like two different colors - they may be different, but together they create a beautiful and colorful rainbow.
298. As the best man, I have to admit the groom has always been the more adventurous one... but I still have better taste in food.
299. Marriage is like a game of poker - sometimes you have to bluff, sometimes you have to fold, but in the end, it's all about the cards you're dealt.
300. The bride and groom are like two different spices - they may be different, but together they create a perfect seasoning.
301. As the best man, it's my job to make sure the groom doesn't get too drunk on his wedding day... but I can't do anything about those shots.
302. Marriage is like a work of art - you have to add different colors, shapes, and textures, but the final result is always beautiful.
303. The bride and groom are like two different animals - they may be different, but together they create a perfect match.
304. As the best man, I have to admit the groom has always been the more charming one... but I still have better dance moves.
305. Marriage is like a game of basketball - you have to work together, pass the ball, and score as a team.
306. The bride and groom are like two different types of wine - they may be different, but together they create a perfect blend.
307. As the best man, it's my job to make sure the groom doesn't get cold feet on his wedding day... but I can't do anything about the weather.
308. Marriage is like a game of chess - sometimes you have to sacrifice a pawn for the greater good, but in the end, it's all about winning the game.

309. The bride and groom are like two different desserts - they may be different, but together they create a perfect ending to any meal.
310. As the best man, I have to say the groom is a lucky guy - he's marrying someone who loves him despite his snoring.
311. Marriage is like a garden - you have to plant the seeds, water them, and watch them grow, but the end result is always worth it.
312. The bride and groom are like two different planets - they may be different, but together they create a beautiful and harmonious universe.
313. As the best man, it's my job to make sure the groom doesn't get lost on his way to the wedding... but I can't do anything about his terrible sense of direction.
314. Marriage is like a game of golf - you have to be patient, take your time, and always aim for the hole.
315. The bride and groom are like two different types of beer - they may be different, but together they create a perfect blend of flavors.
316. As the best man, I have to admit the groom has always been the more stylish one... but I still have better taste in beer.
317. Marriage is like a painting - you have to add different colors, shapes, and textures, but the final result is always beautiful.
318. The bride and groom are like two different planets - they may have different orbits, but together they create a beautiful and unique solar system.
319. As the best man, it's my job to make sure the groom doesn't forget his wedding vows... but I can't do anything about his stage fright.
320. Marriage is like a game of tennis - you have to work together, communicate, and have each other's back, but the goal is always to win.

321. The bride and groom are like two different types of cheese - they may be different, but together they create a perfect pairing.
322. As the best man, I have to say the groom is a lucky guy - he's marrying someone who loves him despite his dad bod.
323. Marriage is like a journey - you never know where it will take you, but as long as you're together, it's always an adventure.
324. The bride and groom are like two different flavors of coffee - they may be different, but together they create a perfect blend.
325. As the best man, it's my job to make sure the groom doesn't spill anything on his suit... but I can't do anything about his clumsiness.
326. Marriage is like a game of chess - you have to think ahead, plan your moves carefully, and sometimes sacrifice a pawn for the greater good.
327. The bride and groom are like two different types of flowers - they may be different, but together they create a beautiful and fragrant garden.
328. As the best man, I have to admit the groom has always been the more outgoing one... but I still have better taste in music.
329. In marriage, it's important to always be open to learning new things. So, [Groom's Name], when [Bride's Name] wants to teach you yoga, just remember to breathe deeply and embrace your inner Zen.
330. The bride and groom are like two different ingredients - they may be different, but together they create a delicious and unique recipe.
331. As the best man, it's my job to make sure the groom doesn't trip on his wedding day... but I can't do anything about those shoes.

332. Marriage is like a dance - you have to be in sync with your partner, follow the rhythm, and always be ready for a spin. 193. The bride and groom are like two different fruits - they may be different, but together they create a perfect smoothie.
333. As the best man, I have to say the groom is a lucky guy - he's marrying someone who loves him despite his terrible sense of humor.
334. Marriage is like a puzzle - sometimes, the pieces fit perfectly, and sometimes you have to try a few different ways to make them work.
335. The bride and groom are like two different seasons - they may be different, but together they create a beautiful and harmonious year.
336. As the best man, it's my job to make sure the groom doesn't forget his wedding ring... but I can't do anything about his nervousness.
337. Marriage is like a game of football - you have to work together, tackle obstacles, and score touchdowns as a team.
338. The bride and groom are like two different types of wine - they may be different, but together they create a perfect pairing.
339. As the best man, I have to admit the groom has always been the more romantic one... but I still have better taste in movies.
340. Marriage is like a journey - sometimes it's smooth sailing, and sometimes it's a bumpy ride, but as long as you're together, it's always an adventure.
341. The bride and groom are like two different pieces of jewelry - they may be different, but together they create a beautiful and unique set.
342. As the best man, it's my job to make sure the groom doesn't get cold feet on his wedding day... but I can't do anything about his nerves.

343. Marriage is like a game of chess - you have to strategize, plan your moves carefully, and always protect your queen.
344. The bride and groom are like two different flavors of tea - they may be different, but together they create a perfect blend.
345. As the best man, I have to say the groom is a lucky guy - he's marrying someone who loves him despite his obsession with video games.
346. Marriage is like a garden - you have to tend to it, nurture it, and give it lots of love, but the end result is always a beautiful and bountiful harvest.
347. The bride and groom are like two different types of coffee - they may be different, but together they create a perfect cup.
348. As the best man, I have to admit the groom has always been the more adventurous one... but I still have better taste in fashion.
349. Marriage is like a game of basketball - you have to work together, pass the ball, and score points as a team.
350. The bride and groom are like two different pieces of art - they may be different, but together they create a beautiful and inspiring collection.
351. As the best man, it's my job to make sure the groom doesn't forget his wedding vows... but I can't do anything about his nerves.
352. Marriage is like a puzzle - sometimes, the pieces fit perfectly, and sometimes you have to try a few different ways to make them work.
353. The bride and groom are like two different types of cheese - they may be different, but together they create a perfect pairing.
354. As the best man, I have to say the groom is a lucky guy - he's marrying someone who loves him despite his snoring.

355. Marriage is like a dance - sometimes it's slow and sensual, and sometimes it's a fast-paced party, but as long as you're together, it's always fun.
356. The bride and groom are like two different types of ice cream - they may be different, but together they create a perfect sundae.
357. As the best man, I have to admit the groom has always been the more organized one... but I still have better taste in beer.
358. Marriage is like a game of chess - you have to be strategic, think ahead, and always protect your king.
359. The bride and groom are like two different types of flowers - they may be different, but together they create a beautiful and unique bouquet.
360. As the best man, it's my job to make sure the groom doesn't have any wardrobe malfunctions... but I can't do anything about those socks.
361. Marriage is like a garden - you have to put in the work, tend to it daily, and appreciate the beauty that grows from it.
362. The bride and groom are like two different types of fruit - they may be different, but together they create a perfect fruit salad.
363. As the best man, I have to say the groom is a lucky guy - he's marrying someone who loves him despite his bad puns.
364. Marriage is like a game of golf - you have to be patient, take your time, and always aim for the green.
365. The bride and groom are like two different types of tea - they may be different, but together they create a perfect afternoon tea.
366. As the best man, I have to admit the groom has always been the more adventurous one... but I still have better taste in wine.

367. Marriage is like a puzzle - sometimes it takes time to find the right piece, but once you do, it fits perfectly.
368. The bride and groom are like two different types of birds - they may be different, but together they create a beautiful and harmonious flock.
369. As the best man, it's my job to make sure the groom doesn't forget his wedding vows... but I can't do anything about his nerves.
370. Marriage is like a game of chess - you have to be strategic, think ahead, and always protect your queen.
371. The bride and groom are like two different types of pizza - they may be different, but together they create a perfect slice.
372. As the best man, I have to say the groom is a lucky guy - he's marrying someone who loves him despite his terrible singing.
373. Marriage is like a garden - you have to plant the seeds, water them, and watch them grow, but the end result is always worth it.
374. The bride and groom are like two different types of beer - they may be different, but together they create a perfect pint.
375. As the best man, I have to admit the groom has always been the more athletic one... but I still have better taste in fashion.
376. Marriage is like a game of tennis - you have to communicate with your partner, work together, and always keep your eye on the ball.
377. The bride and groom are like two different types of dessert - they may be different, but together they create a perfect finish to any meal.
378. As the best man, it's my job to make sure the groom doesn't trip on his wedding day... but I can't do anything about his dancing.

379. Marriage is like a dance - sometimes it's slow and sensual, and sometimes it's a fast-paced party, but as long as you're together, it's always a good time.
380. Marriage is like a science experiment: sometimes there are unexpected reactions, sometimes things get a little messy, but as long as you're wearing your safety goggles and working together, you'll always make a great discovery.
381. They say that marriage is all about communication. So, [Groom's Name], when [Bride's Name] gives you "the look," just remember that it's time to start practicing your listening skills!
382. In marriage, it's important to always be willing to try new things. So, [Groom's Name], when [Bride's Name] wants to experiment with a new recipe, just remember to keep the fire extinguisher handy and enjoy the culinary adventure!
383. Ladies and gentlemen, let's toast to [Bride's Name] and [Groom's Name]. May their love be like a beautiful sunset: full of vibrant colors, inspiring awe, and always leaving you wanting to see it again and again.
384. Marriage is like a game of tug-of-war: it takes strength, determination, and sometimes a little bit of mud-slinging. But as long as you're pulling together, you'll always come out on top.
385. They say that in marriage, you should never go to bed angry. So, [Groom's Name], when [Bride's Name] is upset, just remember to stay up all night and watch your favorite movies together until you both fall asleep.
386. In marriage, it's important to always be each other's rock. So, [Groom's Name], when [Bride's Name] needs a shoulder to lean on, just remember that you're her personal Gibraltar.
387. Ladies and gentlemen, let's raise a glass to [Bride's Name] and [Groom's Name]. May their love be like an evergreen tree: strong, resilient, and always full of life.

388. Marriage is like a game of cards: sometimes you're dealt a great hand, sometimes you have to bluff, and sometimes you just have to play the hand you're dealt. But as long as you're playing together, you'll always have a winning hand.
389. They say that in marriage, it's important to keep the mystery alive. So, [Groom's Name], when [Bride's Name] asks you what you're thinking, just remember that "I was just thinking about how much I love you" is always a great answer.
390. In marriage, it's important to always be prepared for surprises. So, [Groom's Name], when [Bride's Name] comes home with a new plant, just remember to make space in your garden and start practicing your green thumb.
391. Ladies and gentlemen, let's toast to [Bride's Name] and [Groom's Name]. May their love be like a shooting star: bright, dazzling, and always leaving a trail of magic in its wake.
392. Marriage is like a box of chocolates: you never know what you're going to get, but as long as you're sharing it together, you'll always find something sweet.
393. They say that the secret to a happy marriage is to always put your spouse first. So, [Groom's Name], when [Bride's Name] asks you to pick up milk on your way home, just remember that she's testing your dedication to your vows.
394. In marriage, it's important to always be there to catch each other when you fall. So, [Groom's Name], when [Bride's Name] needs a hand, just remember that you're her personal safety net.
395. Ladies and gentlemen, let's raise a glass to [Bride's Name] and [Groom's Name]. May their love be like a blossoming flower: vibrant, fragrant, and always attracting the right kind of attention.

396. Marriage is like a seesaw: it takes balance, trust, and sometimes a little bit of up and down. But as long as you're playing together, you'll always find a way to have fun.
397. They say that in marriage, it's important to be each other's best friend. So, [Groom's Name], when [Bride's Name] wants to have a girls' night out, just remember that you're always invited as her honorary girlfriend.
398. In marriage, it's important to always be willing to lend a helping hand. So, [Groom's Name], when [Bride's Name] needs assistance with a project, just remember that you're her personal handyman.
399. Ladies and gentlemen, let's toast to [Bride's Name] and [Groom's Name]. May their love be like a beautiful piece of art: full of depth, color and always leaving an impression on those who see it.
400. Marriage is like a carnival ride: it's full of excitement, twists, and sometimes a little bit of screaming. But as long as you're holding on tight to each other, you'll always enjoy the ride.
401. They say that in marriage, it's important to always have each other's back. So, [Groom's Name], when [Bride's Name] wants to try a new hairstyle, just remember that you're her personal style consultant and cheerleader.

CONCLUSION

∽

As we reach the end of our humorous journey, we hope that these jokes have provided you with plenty of inspiration and entertainment for crafting the perfect best-man speech. By incorporating a touch of humor, you'll be sure to captivate your audience and create an unforgettable experience for the happy couple.

As you prepare to deliver your best man speech, remember that the key is to tailor the jokes to the personalities and interests of the bride and groom, as well as the unique dynamics of their relationship. Keep in mind that it's essential to strike the right balance between humor and sentiment, ensuring that your speech is not only amusing but also heartfelt and meaningful.

In conclusion, we hope that "Jest in Time: 401 Best Man Speech Jokes to Keep Them Laughing" has equipped you with the necessary tools to create a speech that will be remembered and cherished for years to come. We wish you the best of luck in your role as the best man and hope that the laughter you bring will serve as a testament to the love and happiness that the bride and groom share on their special day.

Printed in Great Britain
by Amazon